Thoughts of My Inner City
An Autobi-oetry

B. Wilder

Free Spirit
PUBLISHING, INC.
Atlanta, Georgia

© 2007 by Brandee George Wilder

All rights reserved
No part of this publication may be reproduced or transmitted in any form or by any means, without written permission of the publisher.

Printed in the United States of America

13-digit ISBN: 978-0-6151-6115-0

PREFACE

Thoughts of My Inner City an Autobi-oetry began its journey over 14 years ago and are a collection of works throughout my childhood into early adulthood. With each poem is a story or observation based on life, love, and the people that have helped to mold me into the person I am today. Though some of the works and characters reflect real life entities, **the focus is on the message** and **not the circumstance**; whether a passing thought, or an event gone past. Each piece is written for the intent of healing and restoration of the human soul. Be blessed.

B.

I KNOW THIS IS A LONG DEDICATION PAGE BUT…..

This book is dedicated to all the people in my life who helped to mold my person, re-construct my broken spirit, nurture my soul, educate my mind and feed my voracious hunger for life; those that hated to love me, didn't know how to love me and those that hated that I didn't love myself. To my husband, Robert, my mom and dad, Pam and George, my sister, Princess, my "mama and daddy", Yvette and Archie, my aunt, Madonna, my aunt, Brenda, my kindergarten teacher, Mrs. Irvin, my best friend, Tiffanie, G-G, Diva, Erica and anyone else that has made a profound impact on my life (you know who you are). Finally, this book is dedicated to the memory of two of the most phenomenal human beings that ever walked the face of this earth; my grandmother, Faye J. Burruss and my "Tio", Rickey W. Greene. Thanks for believing in me, teaching me and guiding me. I know you're looking down from heaven watching over me. I only hope that I can make a difference in this world, like you did in mine. Family and friends……world; Look out because The Best is yet to Come!!!
I Love You Always,
B.

These are the people who made me who I am.

CONTENTS

Inner City Blues	11
For Everything	13
I'll Fly Away	15
Life Lesson	16
Scaling Back	17
Mommy Wasn't There	18
Day After Yesterday	21
Night Life	22
Empty Here	23
She Gave Me All She Had	24
Imagine	25
On A Clear Day	27
It Appeared to Me	28
White Vision	30
What I See Now	33
Truth	36
Silence My Tears	37
Lay My Burdens Down	38
Afraid of Myself	39
From My Roots	41
A Part of Being Apart	42
The Reason Why	44
Granddaddy	46
Soul Sistas	48
"Randa"	50
The Psalm of Brandee	52
Who You Are	53
Mark Anthony	55
Angel of His	56
Dear You	58
Gorgeous George	60
Reflections of Yesterday	62
Lest I Accept Myself	64

Like A Virgin	65
Speckled Pub	67
Soul Eternity	68
Look What You Did	70
Get It Together	71
I Realized	73
Life's Most Dangerous Ride	76
The It of It All	77
Back Down Memory Lane	78
Can I Tell You?	80
Wait and See	81
My Baby	83
C.O.A.L. State of Mind	85
Alpha Male	86
Second Look	88
Not the Same	90
The Seven Wonders	91
Thoughts of the Inner City	92
Only You	94
In the Ship	95
Writer's Vindication	96
Note to Self	98
Strangers in the City	100
Mark the Hour	102

Inner City Blues

Shhhhhhhhhhhhhhhh.
Do you hear the sounds of the inner city blues?
Kids playing,
Mothers praying,
Have you heard the news?
Someone's dying,
A young child's crying,
Teens hip hoppin' and beat boppin'
Raps and rhymes,
Church bells chime,
Old hymns suppressed,
We shall overcome,
Let us march on til the victory is won.

Shhhhhhhhhhhhhhhhhh.
Do you hear the sounds of the inner city blues?
Miss Mary Mack Mack, Mack,
All dressed in black black, black,
'Cause the brother down the street got shot in the back,
People homeless in garbage cans like pigs in a trough,
I can still hear the sounds of that gun going off,
And oh how the screams they ring in my ears,
And mama trying to calm me down,
How can this subside my fears?

Shhhhhhhhhhhhhhhhhhhh.
Do you hear the sounds of the inner city blues?
Double Dutch,
And Hop Scotch,
Kids running up and down the block,

The bounce of the ball on the neighborhood court,
Inner thoughts of a 13 year-old boy selling drugs as his last resort,

Do you hear the sounds of the inner city blues?
Sirens and horns,
Bullets and bass,
And the sound of the raindrops that fall on my face,
And where there is rain,
The children will grow,
And the sunshine will come and bring a rainbow,
Shades of black, white, red, and yellow agree,
And all come together in perfect harmony,
Shhhhhhhhhhhhhh!
Just listen……

For Everything
(For Mrs. Irvin)

For teaching me the fundamentals,
And not just ABC's,
But doing unto others,
As they would do to me,

For quiet time,
And Happy Meals,
And daily show and tell,
And cozy naps,
Afternoon snacks,
And birthday licks as well,

For the joy your smile has brought me,
For the hope your words still bring,
For the blessings you have given,
Not to mention the little things,

For the tears I cried,
That you wiped away with care,
For the times I needed a hand to hold,
And yours was always there,

For challenging me to reach further
And only just believe,
For having faith I could accomplish,
What others could not conceive,

For being who you are,
In spite of all earth's sorrows,
For giving me such hope,
To look forward to tomorrow,

For confidence you had in us,
When down to give a lift,
And teaching us though each one different,
We possessed a special gift,

For all that goes unspoken,
You do at school and home,
I thank God for the Greatest Teacher,
This world has ever known.

I'll Fly Away

When I depart this life one day
And swim that celestial shore,
To live in peace and harmony,
To never die no more,
I'll fly away and be at peace,
Where pain will be no bother,
I'll be the child of The King,
My holy heavenly father,
I'm looking for that blessed day I'll hear my Jesus say,
"Well done my good and faithful child,
With me you'll fly away."

Life Lesson

The journey began long before you said it did,
Never realized the impact birth had until it sank down deep,
Past the mind,
Through the body,
Seeping straight into the soul,
Searching for some prolific revelation to send me to the top,
With candle like aspirations that dwindled with every unmerited
Observation, weakening stare, and criticism,
Was life supposed to cast a sunny gleam on my parade?
Ever thought about being my own sunlight?
The only rain I've found at this point is high expectation from everyone else,
Knowing and seeing diminishes the faith,
And faith obliterated is no hope,
And hope deferred is a dream, never dreamt,
One has to keep steady on the upward trod to success,
In spite of the predestined doubt in the minds of spectators,
For just note, that in the time when your happiness lies in the approval of others,
It isn't your happiness at all,
Life taught me this a few years ago,
And a few years ago before now,
I was a child.

Scaling Back

Is it a crime,
To worth life less than a dime?
And to count death as fiscal,
And beauty less than a nickel,
To degrade ones self for loves sake,
And on a scale of one to ten,
Rate love minus nothing.
Perhaps in vanity love lost its "Romancity",
And I found myself,
Less appealing,
Alone.
Scaling back to where I came from.

Mommy Wasn't There
(For Healing)

I climbed to the highest peak of the tallest tree,
Tumbling to worse than death
Was a trap disguised as a busted knee,

In pain my limbs weak,
The blood gushing everywhere,
I had to ask a stranger for help,
'Cause Mommy Wasn't There.

Around his neck I hung like a slave on a tree,
I wish I'd hung for real if I'd known,
What he was gonna do to me,
Around his sweaty neck and filthy brown shirt I clung,
I was desperate for aid
Somebody's help,
He was the only one,

AROUND

Like a Samaritan doing a Godly deed,
He wiped my welling eyes,
As the trust began to build for him,
He carried me inside,
Just like a "little boy"
My legs scarred and bare,
And then the nightmare commenced,
'Cause Mommy Wasn't There.

Pleading,
"Not on the sofa"
Grandma's brown sofa,

As we staggered through the door,
Struggling to reach down lower to aim the blood down to the floor,
Blood still remnant from the injury before,

"I can't lay on the sofa when my blood is still wet,
Mama warned me before and I'm not off punishment yet.
Please not on the sofa!"
With cold shivers through my body
He began his attack,
It was hard to get my composure lying hostage on my back.

"Mommy! Mommy! Help Me!
I need you Mommy!"
"Shut Up! You keep yelling like that,
And I'm gonna cut you!"
"Mommy!"
"Please girl shut-up!"
Bleeding insides quivering with every single thrust,
"Mama! Mama!"
"Shut-up girl don't you see nobody cares!"
With every single blow received,
'Cause Mommy Wasn't There.

All I wanted was a band-aid,
A gauze to clean and wipe,
But instead he took advantage,
And scarred me for life,

Eternity ended abruptly as I lay in seizure state,
Trembling like December,
My shocked state body quaked,
On both knees numbed and swelling,

My red blood everywhere,
He helped me clean the mess I made,
'Cause Mommy Wasn't There.

Day After Yesterday
(How I Felt)

I can't live here anymore in this vile disgusting place,
Stare at that reflection,
and claim it as my face,
I can't live in peace within with screams echoing around,
The pain inside my soul can't match the pain when I sit down,
I can't close my eyes at night,
Not knowing what's in store,
Lulled by bedtime stories,
I'm not a child anymore,
I can't smile and say I'm happy,
Or sleep and say I rested,
I didn't like myself before and now my worth is lessened,
I can't hold my head up high with teary eyes so drowned,
Without wondering to myself, how could she let me down?
I can't go on anymore appearing to be alive,
Just close the casket now,
'Cause yesterday I died.

Night Life
(For the Sandman)

After dark when everyone was asleep,
I had a second life to keep,
On the outside of home,
Literally looking in,
Couldn't sleep in my room 'cause I was awake within,
Eyelids of lead encompassing my dark browns
Couldn't wait for day to break 'til the day dreams rolled around,
Homeless 'cause I hated home,
But loved to be inside,
Couldn't catch me slipping into sleep,
I kept them open wide,
Unnatural nocturnal creature
Lurking in the dark,
Creating nature's midnight skies
Inside within the dark,
Longing for the day to come so I could see the light,
Like Job in torment constantly,
When day I wished for night,
Death was only scary when I didn't see the fear,
Hope was intangible and dread was always near,
Joy drowned in tears,
Resentment conceiving strife,
These are the reminiscent fragments of the Night Life.

Empty Here
(For the Void)

It's been so empty here,
Alone in my real life,
I had to dream in the day,
And walk the streets at night,

It's been so empty here,
I've been real full of pain,
And the only way to see the rainbow,
Was to look straight through the rain,

It's been so empty here,
No matter how I strived,
Each accolade and note of praise,
Could not keep me alive,

It's been so empty here,
I've closed my eyes to see,
What others said could not be done,
But God helped me achieve,

It's been so empty here,
I went before the fountain,
To fill my pitcher with the faith,
To make it up life's mountains,

It's been so empty here,
I had to trust in thee,
For you're the only one who can,
Fill eternally.

She Gave Me All She Had

Lord I know I'm filthy, worthless than dirty rags,
But through my pain I finally see,
She gave me all she had,
Who am I to say inside that I should not forgive?
Everyday I harbor pain in constant hell I live,
I'm just as sinful as a drunkard, treading hatreds paths,
I'm convinced it is, okay,
She gave me what she had,
I'm falling all apart inside and have need to repent,
The one I should hold in high esteem at times hate and resent,
I'm still angered excessively, I think about the past,
Then the Lord,
Helps me remember,
She gave me what she had,
If Christ marked my iniquity,
I wouldn't stand a chance,
I must remember his divine love,
And take a healing stance,
Just one conversation,
To make my torn heart glad,
I'll tell her I don't blame her now,
She Gave Me All She Had.

Imagine
(For Closure)

Pain no one can imagine,
Holding secrets like a wall,
No one could begin to fathom,
The sharp pains that deranged my mental state of peace,
That deadened my nerve cells,
And like a thief,
Steals my sleep,
Midnights laced in tears for fear of tomorrow from yesteryears events,
And every minute of my life's today,
Stolen sleep,
And relentless repents,
Deadened womb,
Eternal,
Plain as the blood flowing from the fountain of innocence,
And forever repentance,
Imagine,
Sinning that day by default of birth and childhood dreams,
Under cover,
I hid myself inside,
Where the web wove silently and stole my sleep at night,
Bleeding within eternal,
Nocturnally minded to press rewind and relive,
While in forward throttle take what life has to give,
To even me?
Try to erase the pain empathized,
Pinned to the floor,
Screaming,

"I apologize"
Can't Imagine?
Tragic traces of lasting lies,
And dirty lust,
Innocent kisses and vile thrusts,
No longer naïve,
Dirt debris, from rug trodden feet and worn out
hands that shattered
The existing she,
and consolation for busted knees.
Can't Even Imagine.

On A Clear Day

On a clear day,
You can see more than forever,
There's the sun flung so irreconcilably in the sky,
And the stars that shine so gallantly in the night,
And the tears that flow from a human stream,
And the glorious fragrance of the horizon's beam.

On a clear day,
You can see more than forever,
There's the mending of wounded and broken hearts,
The forgiveness of lovers,
And regenerative starts,
And the fresh mist of the flowers bloom in the atmosphere,
And the feeling of completeness,
When genuine love is near.

On a clear day,
You can see more than forever,
There's depth defying effort over weakness and flaws,
And giving more than one has,
When thought they gave their all,
There's seeing good in bad,
When failure is a novice,
And striving for new beginnings,
When the enemy says it's over.

Yes,
On a clear day,
You can see,
Much more than forever

It Appeared to Me

Long the distance seems,
And dim the rays beam.
When we're apart,
Left desolate and incomplete,
Like losing the battle before I start to never victor,
And one figures,
Because the earth tilts,
That pain wilts,
And pedals of insecurity,
Shed light on a universe of darkness,
Slowly desecrated by time,
And imaginations turpentined,
And transformed carnal.
And the Nile between us grows bleak,
As patience grows weak,
And infertility,
Sprouts seeds of impossibility.
Blood loose as web,
Overshadowed by iron tears of pain and despair,
Collectively formed into love by prayer,
And hungry digestion,
Creating obese charity,
Only "He" knows the way unknown,
And hears the silent tone of desperation,
Of disappointment,
And discontentment,
Content being half full,
Never acknowledging the true emptiness that resides,
And pain Oscar nominated hurt hides,
To quench the spirit of anguish that perished,
When He created the greatest treasure,
No meter can measure,

No vessel contain,
No language explain,
That which I esteem a little lower than He himself,
And lower than no being else,
Not even one's self,
Can stand against this force,
That ignites the brightest torch,
Of divine love within my soul,
And to be held and to hold the beat of this heart,
Is to emerge from death to eternal,
Never to depart willingly,
Not even I can sever the ties that bind,
Not even time.
Nor death can untwine,
The bond coagulated in love,
The greatest searcher could never find,
It Appeared to Me.

White Vision
(For the Stereotyped)

So you see,
I'm not who you thought I was,
Because,
I talk proper and correct,
And when you put your money down,
You lost the bet.
A valley girl "Slim and Shady",
Afraid to keep it real,
Cause I look like a girl from California,
Some where in Beverly Hills,
'Cause I talk white,
Act white,
Dress white,
But I'm black in sight from a distance,
Because I drink Evian and Figi instead of faucet water,
And because instead of jumping in the background,
I was talking to the reporter,
When I told you who I was,
You didn't believe me,
'Til you saw me talking to the President on your own T.V.
I guess you had to see it for yourself,
And if knowledge is power,
I'm the Harriet Tubman of words,
But I guess since I'm white,
I'm Zena Princess of Lords,
But I learned my Black History when February came,
And now you "Wanna be Down",
Cause you know my name,
It's not my fault,

I was taught to be me,
That it's Brandee,
With out a Y,
And instead with two ee,
And like a breeze,
I flow with ease,
And little hesitation,
And the hem of my garment needs little alteration,
Yeah my hair is long and real,
It's nice,
It's still hard to maintain,
But I don't have lice,
Who said to be black,
You had to smoke green,
Or eat neck bones at dinnertime with gravy and chit-ter-lings,
Is this the thing that decides my black heritage?
Cause I can trace the Middle Passage through my black lineage.
Do I need scars on my back,
to show the Master's whip,
Or is it apparent in my nose,
Or my slightly wide hips,
The only scars I have,
are the ones from interrogation,
And the only thing that's clear,
Is the mass of hateration,
That you betray,
And game you spit my way,
You say I'm stuck-up and saddity,
Cause you hissed at me,
And because I turned my head,
When you blew a kiss at me,
I don't even know you,
And you don't know me,

I'm running the same race,
Just a little bit faster,
But if you keep trippin' me up,
It's gone be a disaster,
Because we'll both lose,
Because I refuse to let you have your way,
When my ancestors are staring at me from a dark and lonely grave,
And I bet if you looked hard enough,
Instead of driving me insane,
You'd find,
We have some of the same plasma running in our veins,
The way the white slave master raped our ancestors,
Oh, but to say they procreated sounds a whole lot better,
And your "Miscalculation" is not from your friends Expedition,
But it's the beam that's in your eye,
That gives you,
Your "White Vision".

What I See Now
(For Julian)

Your body lying there so still,
Your breath I can feel,
The breath of life that God Almighty breathed into Adam,
and made him a living soul.

The breath he took when he pulled the trigger,
And the smoke of hell,
How did he figure,
He had God's right to take your life.

If I could have taken the bullet,
I promise I would,
But the love that I feel has been misunderstood,
For infatuation,
Because you were a sensation,
To all those,
That had just encountered your articulation,

And like a champ,
I held on til' the very last bout,
But I screamed with painful agony,
When they began to roll you out.

I see it all in the subtle trace,
Of your blackened face,
Where the bullet swiftly left your lifeless carcass,

And such tragedy, never got such reciprocity,
From those around that never saw you at home,
Just knew you were a terror,
When you dove into the in zone.

I sat in your room on that still Saturday,
Waiting for you to bust through the door and say,
Woeday….
Like you would.

And when I went to see your mother,
I didn't know what to say,
Cause we both knew you wouldn't see the same tomorrow,
That I see today,

And like a friend,
I stuck around to the end,
I saw you make the trip from Auburn to Westview,
And the whole time I watched,
I was waiting for you,
To come touch me on my shoulder and tell me to wipe my tears,
But when they put you in the ground,
It triggered all my fears,

Like the trigger he pulled that left you lifeless and mundane,
And now he's running from the sounds of the arthritic pain, and life.
Life, that left that very minute,
That your sin stained soul repented and went to be with God.

Never said goodbye today,
Cause I thought I had tomorrow,
Never sung sad dirges or melodies,
Cause I've never been filled with sorrow,
Like I am from now on,

Til' God calls me home to see my brother,

Times we spent when we were five,
Dreams we'd never get old,
Now I'm sitting here in the kitchen with your mother,
Planning your funeral,
And I tried not to cry,
But when I saw you I hit the floor,
Cause the guy who took your life had never seen you before,

And of all the things I know,
I don't know what to do,
Cause your mother says every time she sees me,
She can't help but see you.
What I see now….

Rest in Peace Julian

Truth

So many times I believed a lie hoping the truth would surface in the end,
Knowing from my teachings Christ has to be the begin,
For it to abide,
But how could I accept that he lied,
Told me to tell her it was my fault,
Tell a story now and forget what I was taught,
Except obey,
Obey him,
Obey God,
Honor and live long,
Lie strong, and,
"I'll never do you wrong cause I'm your friend"
And nobody can love you like I can,
Not no man,
Cause nobody ever done nothing for you,
And just wait 'til I'm through
And you'll see my lie was true,
From the beginning,
Never mind sinning,
Cause God knows your heart,
And from the start,
He put you here to do your part,
That is obey,
Do what I say,
And everything will be okay,
Sure it will,
And once again,
Another lie I told myself to see the truth about my
………friend.

Silence My Tears

Silence my tears because I'm crying out loud in an empty room,
Vexed by the disappointment of life and gloom,

Silence my tears because I'm mortal and weakness is insane,
In a world of tragedy and never ending pain,
'Til eternity

Silence my fear of failure and monstrosity,
Negative reciprocity and reality,

Silence my tears with reality and not dreams,
Like the ray of sun across the horizon beams,
No matter what the season,

Silence my tears and extinguish my anger with truth,
That hate is not learned,
But grown from the root
Purged by jealousy,

Silence my tears of stereotypical perfection,
That outlined the book of my life,
Before I sold the rights,
And cried,
For thirty pieces of silver,

Silence my tears so I can see clearly.

Lay My Burdens Down

Down by my rivers side,
I'll lie what I have to rest,
With hope of lasting happiness,
And love's sweet fragrance caress,

Down by my rivers side,
I'll lay my stubborn pride,
And all the things my natural man
Camouflaged down deep inside,

Down by my rivers side,
There's peace in gentle songs,
Companionship,
And assurance,
I'm safe when I'm alone,

Down by my rivers side,
I'll invite myself to lay,
And watch the currents in my life,
Gently fade away,

Down by my river's side,
That's where I'll firmly stand,
And find relief because I'll know,
Exactly who I am.

Afraid of Myself

Afraid of myself because I'm capable of being a success,
Afraid the ones I leave behind will hate me,
'Cause I wanna be my best,

Afraid to conquer lies,
Because the truth hurts twice as hard,
Living a lie everyday,
And blaming it on God,

Too weak to stand up for myself,
I've hidden behind this mask,
That I'm not good enough alone,
To make my own happiness last,

Afraid my virtue faltered when I said I had enough,
No one saw it killing me,
"Just sometimes life gets rough",
Constantly?

Too tired to start over now,
It's half my life entangled,
Wise enough to acknowledge the problem,
But too foolish to become un-mangled,

Afraid someone will find a treasure,
In what I regard as trash,
So I'll sit around for other's sake,
And see how long I last,
Till it kills me.

Afraid to be a woman,
All He intended me to be,

Not able to give comfort to myself,
But others readily,

Confused,
Scared,
Afraid of Myself

From My Roots

From my roots,
Have sprung many regal bodies,
Royal aura,
Spirit filled,
Sanctified and holy souls,
A legacy of True Holiness passed down through ages I'm told,
If I never knew a single one or shook a single hand,
I know it's rooted down inside and on a Holy Heritage I stand.
From my roots were kings and queens of the Nile,
Escaping to a land of freedom built on faith from kingdoms exiled,
With determined steadfast hope that through anything we would succeed,
As long as we were humbled minded and followed our Saviors lead,
From my roots grew boldness to stand for right through wrong,
And pride to walk in holiness despite traveling alone,
I don't have to know each person, part of this path I stride,
For I feel the presence of their spirit and it keeps my hope alive.

A Part of Being Apart
(For My Mother)

A longtime ago I only dreamed of this moment,
I'd let you have it, then be through,
And not be worried bout you woman.
But you're my mother,
The line of life that composed my existence,
And as much as it used to bother me,
How can I resist it?
That you're my mother,
Nose and all,
Line across,
The pouty lips,
I've been given much in life,
But you gave the greatest gift.
Yes, it's been rough,
But I'm tough,
'Cause you taught me to be me,
When others shunned my disposition,
You cultivated,
Then set it free,
And yes I found it,
After a while,
Seems it all just fell in place,
But it took me by surprise like a slap across my face,
'Cause I was running from the pain that my past felt full of sin,
Till I ran into myself,
And found,
You can't run from what's within,
And that's you,
See I can try with all I muster and my might,
But you'll forever be apart of me,

And I'll never win that fight,
If I forget all that has happened,
I realized I could be free,
I guess I'll just have to forgive you,
Like all the times you've forgiven me.
So I'll deal with my yesteryear,
Its pain, struggles and plenty sorrows,
So I can build on a foundation,
That will support our new tomorrow,
'Cause today I can no longer hide in secret from the truth,
That even when I felt so disconnected,
I was still apart of you.

The Reason Why
(For My Big Sister)

Her majesty rejected,
When your beauty was interjected,
Into the picture that Royalty is,
Your eyes like diamonds freshly cut,
Sparkled in the night,
Inadvertently reversing the day,
And overshadowing the night,
It's your spirit of subtle meekness,
And style of elegance and sleekness,
With bold flavor,
To make onlookers savor,
Your "Regality",
And in reality,
Just a woman striving for perfection,
Sweet in spirit,
Tall in stature,
Yet a rare confection,
To partake,
And with each step you take,
Model mystique seeps from your pores,
And men fling open doors,
And bow at your feet,
To await your arrival,
It's your poise and determination,
That feed your survival,
Long jetted locks,
Laced in waves,
Form a haloed crown,
Giving you what others have found,
To be a reason to hate,
And pecan skin effervescent glow,
Orchestrated ages ago,

By our father,
It's the reference that was given,
When Webster likened loveliness,
It's why others called you just a baby,
And mother named you Princess.

Granddaddy

The only memory I have of you is a picture used to drive,
And stories told by hundreds of people,
Of times when you were alive,
I used to try on an old gray coat,
I heard you used to wear,
And somehow when I had it on,
I felt you were right there.
We never really got acquainted,
You knew of my arrival,
Sometimes I feel if you were around,
You could have aided my survival.
I have the line across your nose,
I wear it as a badge,
That somehow we are one in the same,
This thought, it makes me glad.
Your eyes, I didn't get them,
Although I wish I did,
Maybe God reserved that trait,
To give them to my kids,
I hope He did.
And how you left,
I'm not quite sure,
No one wants to say,
I heard it was so suddenly,
I think,
Was it Labor Day?
I don't know,
I wasn't here,
You left before I came,
But always with me,
A piece of you,
I have your middle name.

I've heard them call you a few things,
There's Gab and Gid, GA,
But nothing would have been as nice to actually
hear me say,
Granddaddy

Soul Sistas

Did you know we weren't blood and never related?
I could have sworn you were my sister,
And all that other stuff was negated,
By the fact that we were siblings bound in foolish actions,
And to know we were the best of friends was the only satisfaction,
I expected,
And was rejected by the notion,
That we were just good friends,
'Til the end,
You'll always be my sister,
Come millions of friends,
Blessed be the tide,
I'm right by your side when I'm needed the most,
Give the maid of honor's toast,
Standing from my seat,
And on my feet to applaud every life event meriting recognition,
Don't need nobody's permission,
To be related,
Not even our mothers orchestrated,
The bond between us real,
And you know how I feel,
'Cause I think you felt it first,
Or worse,
We felt it at the same time,
Like magic,
We waved a wand and became intertwined,
With different minds,
And side kicked into countless hours of tear dropped conversations,
And childlike aspirations,

Sprinkled with the optimism that death could only make us stronger,
And the longer,
I live to learn,
I realize how much I yearned for something I always had,
And now I'm sad, we didn't capitalize on every waking minute,
Whether my house or yours,
My food or your toys,
We we're boys,
Yet we were girls,
How 'bout that sistas from the soul!

"Randa"
(For Miranda Nycole)

Time has flown so quickly since the Lord called you home,
Yet it doesn't ease the void when felt sometimes alone,
To know you left so suddenly,
no chance to say goodbye,
Yet everyday you lived on earth your life did testify,
Of all the things one can accomplish when walking in God's will,
Success is in the deeds fulfilled and not in years outlived,
We never will forget the love you poured through dedication,
To God's house, family and friends and heartfelt recitation,
Your brilliant smile and pleasant aura lingers in the soul,
And will forever be the fragrance I will ever hold,
A day will never pass that a memory be not rekindled,
As long as breath flows through the lungs,
Your legacy will never dwindle,
It's not a matter of time that makes it hard to believe,
That in fleshly nature, your radiant smile,
Or face we'll never see,
We know this life is temporal and no one eternal lives,
But the biggest blow was praying contrary,
To our Father's will,

"Randa", how we love you and praise for having known,
One of the greatest Angels this world has ever known.

The Psalm of Brandee
(For Angela)

In every person's life

At some point,

God sends an angel in the form of flesh

To restore their existence,

Their faith and the essence of which they were.

Living,

Yet dead,

Never alone,

But forlorned,

Aware of my surroundings,

But lost within myself,

I was afforded life,

When I prayed for death.

With a broken heart and spirit my oblations were nonentity,

Intervention guided by divine inspiration

And sincere adoration, by a "Christian"

Gave me motivation to survive.

Grateful am I to the Lord for the love He gave you toward me.

Who You Are
(For Diva)

Mightier than the fortress tall and lancing skies,

It's aura in your sway and the originality captured in your "brown" eyes,

It's A o AKA to strut when you make a subtle move,

'Cause you know you've got the rhythm it takes to back the groove,

It's the presence you command when you stand and grasp attention,

The homage that is given when your name is merely mentioned,

It's the style when you Vogue,

And the Essence of your being,

It's the Vanilla in your complexion but the "Blackness" of your dimension,

It's the compassion in your heart,

But the swagger in your glide,

It's the persona that you carry when you hold your head up high,

Blacker than the roots that anchor your longest strand,

Deeper than the wisdom God gave the wisest man,

It's the gift to teach in precept passed down from our Creator,
It's the "Dee" down deep inside that makes her "Diva Educator",
When times are hard to bear, it's the ease in the mile,
The optimism in your struggle,
Dimpled in your smile,
It's the fuel in your strength,
And your light that shines apart,
It's everything that grace is,
It's simply who you are.

Mark Anthony
(For Deedre)

Mark Anthony as your shinning star,
And Prince of peaceful nights,
The calm in midst of tempests,
And the victor of your fights

Mark Anthony as your cooling waters,
That flow from deep desire,
The wind that blows your storm away,
Yet ignites your deepest fire

Mark Anthony as your jewel,
The vessel that holds the treasure,
To unlock the mysteries of your soul,
And renews your brightest forever

Mark Anthony as the ship,
From which all your trust embarks,
Your strength in fragile hours,
And the light amidst your dark

Mark Anthony as your conqueror,
Which from challenge and despair,
Forged ahead despite adversity,
To obtain you, a gift so rare

"Angel of His"
(For Aunt Madonna)

If I had to describe you,
I just could not begin,
To give a precise synopsis,
From the outside to within,
Your beauty rare and sacred,
A smile pure and divine,
To in detail give reflection,
Would be the infinite of time,
To speak the brightened aura that illuminates your heart,
Could only be a capsule and in regards prove oh so small,
If you knew just how your wisdom,
Has broken studded walls,
And made the least of vessels seem so very tall,
To have knowledge of the strength your loving has provided,
In speaking for a moment,
Seems in God one has confided,
How your spirit so angelic,
Gives aid to wounded souls,
And the mysteries of his love through patience,
In time it too unfolds,
How the meekness of your heart,
Touches the least of men,
How you've touched the quintessence of me,
Without reaching out your hand,
A stern and caring countenance,
Obscured with the past, gives to your loving face,

A glowing, mystic cast,
A laugh lightened softly by a lark-like mellow voice,
And as you sing his praises,
How the heavens all rejoice,
A warm and loving soul,
Abounding in his love,
Sent here on a "mission" 'til your ascension high above,
If one wrote another language,
It still would not possess,
The mysteries of your magnetic force,
Or consecrated loveliness,
And just when at my lowest,
And in uncertainty I dangled,
To let me know there was still hope,
He let me meet his angel.

Dear You
(For Brandon)

Dear You,
It was the hardest I had ever seen her push without
our help,
I knew it was a different love,
She wasn't doing it for herself.
With one deep breath,
and a stream of silent prayers,
We held hands and with one strong command,
you were lying there.
So tiny and feeble,
through teary eyes I saw,
that with everything she had,
in that moment you became her all.
And I couldn't help but feel the power of the bond
we formed,
almost instantly as I held you,
so frail within my arms.
I didn't know it possible,
but in one minute of time,
I had fallen deeply in love and you weren't even
mine.
What an experience it was,
how her deeds had changed my life,
God took my worldly love,
and gave me a completely different kind that night.
I was speechless and for once there was nothing I
could do,
I stood there so meager me,
beholding such an enormous you.
Such a task of enormity,
put into our small hands,
Once a land of many strangers,

now a village to raise this man.
And so tonight when I kneel,
I'll think of only you,
as I thank my God above,
for such a beautiful nephew.

Gorgeous George
(For My Daddy)

It was coming home at 4 A.M. with no shoes on your feet,
'Cause you sold them to pay the light bill,
And to buy us food to eat,
That was Gorgeous to me.

And for bringing ice pops to our room when mama said to whip us,
And giving me a dollar for baby teeth,
And every time I had the hiccups,
That was Gorgeous to me.

For hocking your car to pay the past due bills,
And standing outside to catch a ride,
Amidst the freezing chill,
That was Gorgeous to me.

And for making a Christmas fireplace cause we couldn't afford a tree,
And eatin' bologna and vanilla wafers for dinner,
So we could have Mickey D's,
That was Gorgeous to me.

For using Royal Crown to grease my face and ponytail,
And going to 3 different grocery stores for Red Rock Ginger Ale,
Cause my tummy ached,
That was Gorgeous to me.

And riding me on your leg like a cowboy going to town,

And for making me laugh when I was mad,
Saying "We don't want your kind around."
That was Gorgeous to me.

For teaching me how to make a dollar out of only
15 cents,
And getting my "hustle" on selling ties, shirts and
homemade cufflinks,
Cause I needed money for church,
That was Gorgeous to me.

And for just being my daddy,
With our matching eyes and hair,
And knowing I could call for help and you'd
always be there,
No matter what others may say,
And look at you and see,
I'll always remember the things you did,
That's why you're Gorgeous to me.

Reflections of Yesterday
(For the Realization)

As I stare steady nostalgic,
Image glistened like stars in midnight air,
It's hard to recognize the face,
Wrinkle traced,
Color hidden gray strand hair.

Taken back to times of pageants,
Beauty and crowned for sight,
How fast the times though hard often in my life,
Flew by like daybreak light.

The mole that wasn't a couple of days before
Creeping to surface like nights' unexpected fall,
And the radiance of my youthful existence doesn't exude at all,
Maybe a little,
Though in proportion,
very small.

Staring closely at the figure for some abrupt,
dramatic change,
I noticed though the time had passed,
My image remained the same,
This revelation for me is strange.

Sun kissed, naturally dark hues pigment my yellow skin,
For then,
I searched inside the reflection to retrieve the girl within,
In sin,
I longed to see yesterday.

And slowly as morning rolls around my thoughts
come to end in place,
Where I rise from slumber to find in reality,
What I saw was my mothers face,
Looking within without reason,
And awed with disbelief,
I realize now the reflection shown,
Was who,
I'll one day be.

Lest I Accept Myself

Lest I accept myself,
Ain't gon' be no success in store,
Lest I accept myself,
Ain't gon' be no love like neva before,
Lest I accept myself,
Ain't nobody gon' like me either,
Lest I accept myself,
Ain't gon' have no bright future,
Lest I accept myself,
Ain't gon' have no child to give birth,
Lest I accept myself,
Ain't neva gon' see my worth,
Lest I accept myself,
Ain't gon' quit my sins,
Lest I accept myself,
Ain't neva gon' be no true friend,
Lest I accept myself,
Ain't neva gon' live for real.

Like A Virgin

I wish I could say it's new,
Cause there's the borrowed and I'm feeling blue,
But what's the use?
The truth is, I'm not,
I heard it before it wasn't my fault,
But just because I didn't give it,
Doesn't mean it isn't lost,
Please don't try to coax me,
I've lived a lie long enough,
I know that life's not fair,
I guess that junks just tough,
That I won't walk down the aisle snow white veiled in serenity,
Cause in my childhood I was robbed and stripped of my virginity,
Try peace of mind,
Quiet hours,
Self-acceptance, all the things,
That no dress or fancy flowers,
Not the most expensive ring,
Can restore,
So much more,
I lost in just one fall,
When I gave a little trust,
And in return he took it all,
Speaking frankly,
I see it plainly,
That nobody knows what to do,
So just be happy I'm still breathing and finally made it through,
I'm just imagining what it feels like to completely forgive your sins,

And to know because "It's not your fault" you will walk down,
Like a virgin.

Speckled Pub
(For O)

In you was the vision of inner solitude,
Wrapped in hope and winding beautifully across
the horizon like a rainbow,
Unsuspecting like its end with no illusions
Just hope filled potted aspirations,
Like a cast stone with no definite destination,
You skipped and leaped across the tempestuous
waters of life,
Into a sea of self expectation and examination,
Until landing as if guided by the windmills of your
mind to an off shore place,
Situated in an inward island of peace,
Knowing that the journey,
Which once was an exploration
To prove the world was rounded to the point of
equality,
Was now a resting place to harvest the fruits of
your labor,
And yet in all the glistening points of your diamond
like precision,
The pub will always be your cornerstone,
For it was being speckled with the debris of life,
That gave you your first brilliance.

Soul Eternity

Forever is much shorter, when blinded by deceit,
Feasting, consumed a life in sin,
Your soul's eternity,
Wilt thou spend a season,
Pleasure laden in damnation,
A sacrilegious creature fit for your father Satan?
Repentance grieved His spirit when his likeness we betrayed,
And wished Him being omnipresent, He never would have made,
Us, in Their image,
Yet in greed sewing seeds and fertile lies,
In destitute state of soul and spirit,
He still will hear our cry,
If, we confess, and live true to what we should believe,
For wages passed for deeds done now,
Your soul's eternity,
He doesn't hear a Sinners prayer,
Stop echoes empty rumble,
Wails of pain, grief and sin,
To the bottomless pit they tumble,
Reunion with such hollow utterance,
Inevitable less, vague cries,
For God is not a man, His rewards make Him no lie,
Too late is only sure when you give Him back the ghost,
And ponder if in life gone past you rendered Him your most,
Live if only for Him now,
You'll reap continuously,
For in all that you have sewn and more,

Your Soul's Eternity.

Look What You Did

You let her lay with a man,
To gain a status promotion,
With no regard for your child,
Her thoughts,
Her soul,
Or emotions,

You really don't care what she had to do,
To live or simply eat,
Laid down more than just principles,
Had to lie, steal and cheat,

You let her do it any way,
Because it would profit you,
Just let her be a worthless item,
No matter what she had to do,

You turned your head and let them use her,
Knew she felt violated,
And instead of being a father,
You readily instigated,

You denied her in the face of trouble,
To save your own reputation,
And didn't give another thought,
To her indignation,

And now so many years have passed,
The scars have yet to heal,
Her life is marred by degrading memories,
Just Look What you did!

Get It Together
(For the Mistreated)

People act like it's the greatest,
And that everything is swell,
From the angle that I'm standing from,
Man love,
It burns like hell,
When you've given all you've got,
Just to find it was for nothing,
While the whole time you've been building,
He's been steadily de-constructing,
Cutting down your spirit and the person that you are,
I know it's different when you're "In it" but I'll never get that far,
You say I should be happy,
Because he doesn't beat you,
If you think that it's a privilege,
Maybe someone really needs to,
Slap some sense in your head,
And make you see the truth,
That your man's only a reflection of what you allow him to do,
'Cause I'd die before he beat me,
And choked before I cried,
To have him treat me like I'm nothing,
And call me everything but,
A child of God,
I'm just saying,
Maybe you should rethink this,
And see where your mind is it at,
Is it that you really love him?
Or how you feel,
When he's got you on your back,

Any man can caress you,
And undress you all night long,
But it takes a real man to love you,
For the things that have gone wrong,
In your life,
Instead of using that as an excuse,
For abuse,
And try to make things right.
I know life's not perfect,
Roses still have thorns,
And the wounded still have nerves,
But it's all in how you view yourself,
And what you think you deserve,
Good women are a commodity,
God's greatest and rarest treasure,
Stop rumbling through the trash and
Get it Together!

I Realized
(For Old Times Sake)

You know the other day,
I came to the conclusion,
That the love that I had must have been an illusion,
I just understood for the first time we were always on different levels,
Whether I was behind and you were in front, the point is, that we were never, together,
But it's okay, I learned to deal with the snickers, the smirks and the stares,
The loving you until it hurt and not knowing you didn't care,
Were you ashamed?
I don't know.
Did we play games?
I can't remember,
We had fun,
Or was I the only one that knew it was "meant" to be?
All the close calls, and steady stares, were only a figment of my imagination,
And the sensations,
Quirked by elation,
Was only a thin client to my naivety,
I knew, I just didn't care enough to see what was always blindly staring back at me,
No love,
Not from you at least,
I never really spoke my peace,
Surprised?
Don't be,
Maybe your mama should have told you how to love,

When she was giving you a shove,
Into the other direction,
Insurrection with a license,
As long as the tone remained neutral,
Cause you were too young to love faithfully,
And yet remained a virgin,
In spite of me,
Wasn't my fault we weren't encouraged to love each other,
Not by others,
I motivated myself because I didn't want to see you with anyone else,
It was the music between us that soothed my soul,
And gave birth to new ideas in droves,
In the zone,
All alone,
On the phone,
I was apart of you when there was no connection,
Got heated next to you when there was no convection,
Stood proud when you stooped in the corner afraid,
'Cause I was happy in my heart about the progress we'd made, since child hood,
At least as a kid I felt good,
You were chunky,
But my monkey and we swung together,
'Til others saw your beat,
And you lost some weight and picked up your feet,
To walk in a different direction at the discretion of your family,
Ain't gone never be another to love you like me,
I don't care what they say,
I loved you my way,
And I got nothing,

But a very important lesson that will last me 'til I die,
Worth every tear I cried,
Deserving and undeserved,
Audible and every unspoken word,
I got a friend,
I think,
Out the situation,
As long as I keep things in perspective and don't get caught up in elation,
'Cause when we gather in "Convention" maybe not by intention,
I'm not needed to next Tuesday's,
And all those feeling used days,
Just disappear as reality fades into a dream,
That maybe I just never should've dreamt,
No hard feelings cause I know charity in the most divine way,
And still listen reluctantly to every word you say,
Because I care,
But be aware there's a difference in my feelings,
And now I've finally realized that's the way we love,
But I'm cool with that now.

Life's Most Dangerous Ride

Lanes that leap like cars on a busy freeway,
The easy way is to take the next exit,
But charity does the best thing.
That's the scenic,
Show you mean it,
Full of hope and precision,
And selfishness causes heart collisions,
And homicidal erosion of the heart,
Like a car in park,
On the busiest highway,
And my way,
Full of sideway streets of lies, envy, deceit, and desperation,
Infidelity leaving bittersweet melodies,
From north to south in a crowded nation,
Lonely yet not alone,
Alone but not by myself,
Cause there's a passenger next to me beating ten times faster,
Than life ends,
That's reality,
Love's not promised to end in "P",
But often interrupted abruptly in "D",
Like dead to the world because of the pain,
That love gained,
The weights of depression that pound my bleeding heart,
And no transfusion,
Can reverse the disillusion,
done to betray my perception.
To start again,
I take another course,
To love myself first.

The It of It All

The fiber of my total existence in sickness and in health,
In poverty and in wealth,
At life's deepest depth,
That's where I'll be,
On dry land,
Or the red sea,
Only the omnipotent can divide me and you,
Whatever we go through,
That's what It is
Strong because I am,
When light I see the dark,
Dangers shadow our narrow paths,
On life's journey we embark,
Separation never a thought,
Proud I stand stalk,
In the middle of death,
That's where It is,
Aisle laced in virginity,
Sweet serenity,
In wisdom,
Ignorant of tomorrow,
Never mind the sorrows,
Treading pedals and lighting candles to brighten the future,
That's where It will be,
When oldness becomes new,
Roses turn blue,
Night is never and ignorance is clever,
Whatever,
Together,
We will be lovers forever,
The It of It all.

Back Down Memory Lane
(For My Mom)

Mom,
Remember when you used to do my hair in a thousand braids?
And I got sea sick from all those waves,
and the smell of pink moisturizer that drizzled down my face?

And it was a sad thing when it was time to go to bed
Cause you were done plaiting that last braid on my head,
And I wanted to stay up with you and watch Ginger and Fred, in *Top Hat*.

But forget that,
It was *Daddy Long Legs* with Leslie and Fred,
Or *Mary Poppins* and *The Sound of Music* that still plays in my head,
All those memories that no one can erase,
Traits that make us so much alike that have nothing to do with our face,

But I was still offended when someone mentioned that she looked more like you than me cause we were both "yellow"
Couldn't they see?
That I was more your twin than she.

I may have had daddy's forehead and big brown eyes,
But he and Princess were red and me and you were the same color when we were standing side by side,
Even had the same line across our nose,
Smirking smile and moles, on the corner of our lips and I'd pout mine and make it stick out a bit to really look like you.

Remember Adams Park and swimming?
Hardee's and chocolate vanilla swirls,
Roast beef sandwiches when I ate meat
And all of us asking for more,
And you and Auntie Barbara scrapping up to buy another curly fry,
What sweet mommy's you were with your van load of kids.....

And why you'd buy such nice things
For your girl that "should have been a boy"
I would have been content with just a toy,
But you thought that Shirley Temple curls and patton leather shoes would refine me,
But for some reason you just couldn't confine me with lacey gloves and crinolines

Then again,
Those whippings for scuffin' up my shoes might have done the trick,
I don't know, but I remember getting my share of licks.

Remember dance recitals and tutus?
Emergency room visits and all the boo boos,
That were mended with rubbing alcohol and dumdum lollipops?

The daily stops by the library to rent a movie or a book,
And they may not have wanted to watch,
But for hours we would sit,
And watch old movies with Doris Day or something good on AMC,
But you'd cover my eyes when they'd kiss,
"Cause I was too young to see".

Those were the good ole days,
When I was a kid and could play all day,
Yep, Thanks for the trip down memory lane.

Can I Tell You?

Can I tell you how much I dig you?
I mean, dig deep into your soul,
Through those piercing dark brown eyes,
Can I tell you I'm mesmerized by that dimpled reflection in your smile?
Can I tell you that all the while,
I'm thinking that maybe,
I'll just one day have your baby,
When we walk down the aisle,
And become one?
Can I tell you my life has just begun to see you and I apart,
To start,
Over from the beginning?
Can I tell you the urge I have to keep from sinning is so amazing,
The desire to keep the fire pure,
How in spite of doubt I see right through.
Can I tell you I want it to be new,
For me and for you?
Can I tell you I love the very core of your soul,
Down to your toes,
And every night I kneel,
How I yield to God's will that one day again,
You and I will be we in Holy matrimony.
Can I Just Tell You?

Wait and See

In the distance of your mental you're pondering my intentions,
our love surreal, no man thought this invention,
can unfold the mystery we hold in tomorrow,
Right this minute, and in an instance,
I become yours for always,
counting down the days,
'til we engage,
Engaged licensed to die daily in each other's arms,
from all harm,
And never let go intentionally.
Space only creates the focus,
to notice, the love exuding natural.
And even though the physical we don't attack,
know you touch me deeper than any physical contact,
Like a lever pulled and desecrated time,
you send me to higher levels when you elevate my mind,
How did it happen we ask, in a silent steady stare,
One day you were my brother and I thought you didn't care,
I didn't.
And now yesterday is oh so much farther away,
I can't see from behind, how this love appeared fogs my mind,
But it's okay 'cause I live for day,
Or' night falls when no man can work and in the seclusion doubts and fear lurk,
It's complicated,
PG, X-rated respect,
Given nourishment to feed your spiritual intellect,
While all the while in tact,

Know you got my back,
'Til forever turns into from now on,
How long?
Not long,
Still strong?
I do you wrong?
Never.
Not to hurt you within,
and I figured out our love is perhaps our deepest sin,
Just love Him too, like I love you, and boy I'm through,
Marry you? Never maybe,
Have your baby?
Anything, nothing withheld,
Walk through hell,
Steam the floods,
Give my blood,
If you'd only love Him free, like you love me.
We'll Wait and See

My Baby
(For My Husband)

There was never a question of Black or White when
I was with you,
Maybe right or wrong,
Depending on the tone,
I only knew with each stroke,
My body went into choke,
And chills up and down my spine,
Never a question of time,
We could take it fast or slow,
I was willing to go high or low,
As long as you went with the flow,
Never had much experience,
Just knew how it should sound,
So I faked it sometimes until I came,
Pound for pound,
To your level,
But with each caress,
I began to know your sacredness,
To appreciate who you were,
And at the end of each encounter,
Dig a little deeper to learn the right form,
It was an art I hadn't treasured,
But I slowly learned I needed to measure,
Each beat of your heart,
as I moved to our melody with each start.
You tickled my Fancy.
Others knew I was inexperienced,
But didn't feel what I felt,
Half as much,
Each time we touched,
Even made me relax my shoulders and take a deep
breath before I approached you

And tried again to do it right,
And I could go all night,
Like to do it without the lights,
'Cause I was ashamed of my bodily form,
The curves weren't right,
And my posture wasn't correct,
I knew I had to get toned,
'Cause you always stood erect,
And correct,
Even if I was wrong,
You were that way all night long,
And we could do it 88 ways for days,
If I knew the right position and composition to
carry us both through,
Just had to keep my focus on you,
No matter what was going on,
And when I mastered sitting,
I could stand and you stay low and let me flow,
Just do my thing,
all over you.
So gentle,
Yet so sleek,
So rugged,
Yet so meek,
So mild,
So sharp,
So dark,
So…..
You,
Some call you Boston, Petrof, Bishop and
Newmann,
They can call you what they like,
You're still my Baby Grand!

C.O.A.L. State of Mind
(For That Cat)

Ya know,
They say it takes a million years for one piece to
transform into an alternate state of diamond like
resilience,
and the pressure applied gives way to precise
angles of unimaginable brilliance.
And though it's only been since I was 8,
I'd wait more than a million years to be your
diamond,
for the rest of my life.
And that hope,
is the pressure applied,
Kneeling in prayer and standing silently in your
corner,
as you live on to attain your highest grade.
Seems at this point in our lives,
we both seek clarity.
And while I know that the true color of our
friendship is love,
until I come forth as the jewel of your eye,
I'll keep my treasure hidden with a coal state of
mind.

Alpha Male
(For the Greek)

Boy you work it well in your regal Black and Gold,
Had it going on before,
But now,
You've exceeded the Goal,

Your smile is like a beacon,
Bringing ships to safely dock,
If I was sailing in your direction,
Boy I'd surely stop,

Your style and your charisma,
Are only a minor touch,
And don't captivate your audience,
Nearly half as much,
As your smile,

And all the while,
You strut humbly to your destination,
And got me thinkin' to myself,
How can we be related?
Like forever,

It's so serious what you've done to my ego,
You're the beginning of my thoughts
And I made you half to my equal,

You can teach me what you like,
And I'll pay close attention,
'Cause your eyes are working overtime,
And your swagger we won't even mention,

But the entity that makes you everything,

Is knowing you possess,
Such a sweet and caring disposition,
Carved intact with pure finesse.

I don't think you understand that this revelation is
for real,
So I'll let it marinate a while,
'Til it's clear just how I feel,

So keep strutting how you do,
But let it be real understood,
That I completely foster your beliefs,
And am down for the brotherhood!

Second Look

Look at me,
Straight in the eye,
Do I seem stressed and distraught?
That my mothers were beaten, raped, molested,
Abused, oppressed and bought.

Do I look like I go lacking?
When you attempted to inflict the worst,
Tried to starve me of my dignity,
But it's for humility now I thirst.

Look at me,
Face to face,
A smile of warmth,
Should I be cold?
At the thought that all my children were harassed,
Beset and sold.

Did you think that I would carry
Such a load as great as hate?
I'm still tryin' to bear the burden,
Of the shackles heavy weight.

Look at me,
Study hard how I protect with my own hands,
All the Lord blessed me to acquire,
While I was tending to your land.

Does it bother you so greatly,
That I lived to see the day,
Where I walked around freely,
No reserves or tied restraints?

Take a long hard look,
Because I've moved on with the past,
And if you stop looking at my color,
You'd see your equal at second glance.

Not the Same

Remember what I was when we met long ago?
I didn't know my purpose,
Had very far in life to go,
Remember how I carried myself,
Needing no one's help?
In need of humbleness of mind,
Not embracing each new step,
But God since then has abased me down,
Turned my existence inside out,
To teach me what real livings' about,
Things have changed I'm not the same,
I live now steadfast in my Father's name,
Just think back on things I said that I would never do,
For in my lowest hour it was He that brought me through,
And while you're looking on the outside for some abrupt dramatic change,
Know it's on the inside that my living's not the same.

The Seven Wonders

One, the Master's presence,
To comfort and console,

Two, a broken spirit,
With faith to ease the soul,

Three, the inhibition,
That life is not my home,

Four, the reassurance,
I'm never here alone,

Five, a glaring smile,
Behind a broken past,

Six, determination,
To make happiness last,

Seven, awareness,
I'm not a little girl,

These are,
The Seven Wonders,
The Seven Wonders of My World

Thoughts of the Inner City

What exactly is an Inner City Youth?
Am I Inner City because I live in the city?
or because the city lives inside of me?
Is it the complexion of my skin?
Or the complex that lies within?
Is it the way I walk?
The way I talk?
The dreams I dream?
Or just the reality that I live in,
The reality that being proper,
Is "pro-white",
And being Ghetto,
is getting somewhere.
What about the kids that live in the suburbs far
beyond the out skirts of town,
Are they Inner City or Inner Suburb?
Some people say because I pronounce all the
syllables in my words that I'm trying to be someone
that I'm not,
Maybe it's that I'm being all that I am, or have ever
been taught to be,
Maybe it's not the city,
Maybe it's the state itself,
The state of mind that everyone seems to be in,
That being well spoken,
well versed,
well educated,
well written
and well rounded,
Is well……
Not normal for someone of my "caliber".
Why is it that being Right,
Is so Wrong,

And being so weak,
Is so strong,
Inner City,
Inner City Youth,
It's something to think about.

Only You

Only you can make a losing thought win,
Only you can purify the filth and obliterate the sin,
Only you can take a dream and make it true and real,
Only you can cease the storm or command the earth stand still,
Only you can blot the past and rectify the spirit,
Only you can hush the evil thought and still be near to hear it,
Only you can heal the tattered soul and restore its' former state,
Only you can take the smallest man and make his deeds seem great,
Only you,
Only you

In The Ship

My feet are shod in the gospel of peace,
Going to live for the cause, or die in the least,
I'm ready to lay it down to take my faithful reign,
As long as I live for God,
I'll die in Jesus' name.
I'm armed in the breastplate of his holy righteousness,
And when my work is done,
I'll lay it all to rest,
I only see the living,
For the world can do no harm,
When I'm ordered in his steps,
I'm encamped within his arms.
My faith so valiant shields the trials this world may place,
I'll endure the toils and pain,
For just one single taste,
I'm anchored in his promise and seeking for my soul,
And wouldn't trade one single trial for all the wealth untold.
I'm fighting for my everything,
And Satan's snares prove ripe,
But as long as I stay in the ship he cannot touch my life,
So I'll fend the angry storms and lest I faint or slip,
I'm going all the way with Christ for He is in the ship.

Writer's Vindication

When I say what's on my mind,
Nobody can hear me,
'Cause I do it,
So when I'm through it,
Nobody is offended,
I send it,
To the uttermost points of my core,
So I can know exactly what's in store for my renaissance,
And what I want is to free myself from what's plaguing me,
Cleanse myself from what's weighing me,
Down,
It may sound crazy to you,
But I'm not talking in your direction,
So you can just step off my conversation,
Do you feel me?
You can't hear me,
'Cause I'm not talking to you anyway,
Yet you hear every word I say,
Not a tone uttered,
Or an eyelid batted or shuttered,
'Cause you know to keep your focus in my vicinity,
And there's plenty you could learn from me,
Yet still I care what message my healing sends,
Even though not long ago,
No one cared about the hell I lived in,
Yeah for real,
If you'd just free your mind to the point,
To be bound by my words,
'Cause that's the only thing that could possibly disturb,
You,

'Cause I'll never say one word,
Just remember what you heard,
From the peanut gallery,
And make no mistake,
That my content strictly lyrical gives plenty
nourishing intake,
'Cause I gave to self first,
'Cause I thirst, for wordage worthy of my approval,
Believe It.

Note to Self

Just let it go for a minute and put down the mask,
No fake smiles or solemn speeches,
It's okay to be sad,
Just be human,
You can do it,
There's nobody here but us,
You and I,
We and me,
No reason not to trust,
There's nothing more to lose,
You already won the bet,
Kept a smile, gave a speech,
They never saw you sweat,
Between us two, just me and you,
I know it's got to be taxing,
To appear relaxing,
Struggling to keep your head above the tears,
Looking forward trying hard not to dwell on the years,
Your biggest fear,
Needing help cause you've always wanted to be consoled,
Now it's hard to have that child like faith,
You feel you've gotten too old,
And life's harm,
Was comforted by your own arms,
And that pain that lingers,
The tears cried and then dried with your own fingers,
Deeply seeded in self denial,
Standing guard like on trial,
Okay, give it up,
You've already won your case,

Erase that smile off your face,
That was painted by determination,
To never deal with life's situations,
Until convenient for everyone else,
It's okay to be angry but don't harbor it within,
The longer the cancer festers,
The more dangerous becomes the sin,
I know you want to,
Cry a tear or two,
If not for me,
Do it for you,
Better yet do it for us both,
Give some sign of hope, that you understand,
When do you let go of others and hold your own hand?
Just thought I'd ask,
Wondering how much longer you can last,
Being someone everybody knows,
Except you,
Okay I'm through,
Nothing else.

Sincerely,
Self

Strangers in the City

There are many strangers in this city where I dwell
that used to be my friends,
Ones I took sweet council with,
Shared dreams and for countless hours we'd sit and
commune together
As life mates,
Not like on dates or for being in love for eternity's
sake,
But being friendly like sticking closer than a
brother,
But I've found that sometimes you have to be a self
lover,
To survive the blows that life brings about as a
result of being blinded to the state of foolishness,
Being too young to be an old fool and too old to be
truly naïve,
How did this happen to me?
Cause I was young

A young one,
A lonely child,
A wild child,
Hungry for attention and resenting contention,
Reaching out to whatever hands dropped low
enough within my reach.

There are many strangers in this city where I dwell
that used to be my friends,
Ones I said would always be there
And now I realize that there are many seasons to
life,
Those you don't even learn about until you're in the
middle of the sweltering inferno of betrayal
wearing goulashes and there's no rain in sight

Until you open your eyes and see that "they were just using me"
And instantly dressed to weather every cold shoulder,
The tears 12 inches to every foot fall harder and faster than you could have ever imagined,
Making up for the deficit that has long caused your heart to be dry

My, my, my,
How hard it is to grow up and leave the past behind,
But I've got to forget those things which were,
To focus on all I see ahead because there are new persons sojourning this way.
But I'll be careful who I entertain,
For I don't want to get acquainted with being hurt,

Not in my city,
Not where I dwell,
Because in my city,
It's just me………
And occasional company.

Mark the Hour

Today,
Right now,
In this single moment,
I fell in love with myself,
Yes,
I finally saw past the void and the pain
And managed to like the image chiseled ill fatedly and plain,
And I'll remain the same for this point and time,
Because I see me,
For what I really am,
No, I didn't erase the hurt,
Or dilute the shame,
but the revelation that I'm human just occurred to me.
The idea of taking life minute by minute for one single second,
has soothed an aching sector of my spirit.
Just for today,
For now,
I'm grateful for the past.
And maybe tomorrow,
I'll hate the thought of the future,
But since it never comes anyway,
I'll deal with tomorrow,
When it gets here.
Mark the hour,
For today I learned to live with myself.

www.ingramcontent.com/pod-product-compliance
Lightning Source LLC
Chambersburg PA
CBHW051707040426
42446CB00008B/756